Nathan Levy's

STORIES WITH HOLES
VOLUME 1
Revised & Updated
By Nathan Levy

A collection of original thinking
activities for improving inquiry!

An N.L. Associates, Inc. book

T0204352

N.L. Associates, Inc.
PO Box 1199
Hightstown, NJ 08520-0399

Library of Congress Catalog Number
89-92195
ISBN 1-878347-66-7

Printed in the United States of America

i

PREFACE – by Nathan Levy

This book is the result of several years' accumulation of ideas leading to puzzling stories that lend themselves to what I call thinking games. The "games" have become the means for thousands of people to carry on a totally enjoyable process of engaging critical and imaginative thinking. Volume 1 of my <u>Stories with Holes</u> is a collection of stories that has been gathered from various sources. <u>Nathan Levy's Stories with Holes Volumes 2-20</u> are original. Wherever I speak I share some of the stories with my training groups. Teachers, parents and children enjoy the stories immensely. I hope you will as well.

INTRODUCTION

The objectives of using <u>Nathan Levy's Stories with Holes</u> include the following:

- to provide for growth in imagination and intuitive functioning
- to give experiences that display the fun of working cooperatively, rather than competitively, on a common problem
- to increase cognitive skills of resolving discrepancies through successful experiences
- to provide enjoyable changes-of-pace for task-oriented learning environments

This is a structured activity. It is designed to ensure involvement on the part of each participant, and to promote feelings of group and individual success.

The games are designed to accommodate all levels. "Children" from ages 8-88 will benefit from using these stories.

The time a story takes will vary. Usually a story lasts from 3 to 30 minutes, but some stories can take days. Children, lower grades through high school, tend to regard these thinking games as play instead of work. It is one of the few activities I know of that "hooks" almost anyone into creative use of their intelligence, i.e. learning, almost in spite of themselves. Nathan Levy's Stories with Holes are for all groups over age seven, regardless of background or achievement level.

**Please note that I have revised the above introduction and the following methodology from the way they appeared in the original collection of Stories with Holes. The revisions are based on my current workshop experiences with children and adults.

N.L.

iii

METHODOLOGY

The first time a group plays, it will be necessary to begin by announcing something like the following: "I am going to tell you a story with a hole in it – I mean that an important part of the story is missing. Listen carefully so you can find the missing part, for the story may not seem to make much sense to you at first…"

At this point, tell the story once, pause, and then tell it the same way again. Then say…

"You can ask questions that can be answered either with a "yes" or with a "no". I can only answer "yes", "no", "does not compute", or "is not relevant". If I answer, "does not compute", that means that the question you asked cannot receive a straight "yes" or "no" without throwing you off the track."

Allow for questions about the process, if there are any, but usually it is best simply to jump into the game by having the questioning start. The process becomes clear as the game progresses. Once a group has played the game, the full directions given above for playing the game are unnecessary.

From this point on, answer only in one of the four designated ways. The following is an example of a computed story taken from <u>Stories with Holes</u>, and how it might be played:

Story: Mitch lives on the twentieth floor of an apartment building. Every time he leaves, he rides a self-service elevator from the twentieth floor to the street; but every time he returns, he rides the same self-service elevator only to the fifteenth floor, where he leaves the elevator and walks up the remaining five flights of stairs. Repeat, then ask who knows the answer already; if any do, ask them to observe and not give away the answer.

Question: Does the elevator go all the way up?
Answer: Yes.
Q: Does he want the exercise?
A: No.
Q: Does it have something to do with the elevator not working right?
A: No.
Q: Does he have a girlfriend on the 15th floor who he stops to see?
A: No.
Q: Does he have something different about him?
A: Yes.
Q: Is he a robber?
A: No.
Q: Is he a real person?
A: Yes.
Q: A tall person?
A: No.
Q: Is his size important?
A: Yes.
Q: I know! He's too short to reach the button!
A: Right!

v

At this point, make certain that all the participants understand the answer and why it is the correct answer. In the example given above, the group found the answer quite soon. Instead of starting a new game -- particularly if this is the first time playing – spend some time processing the game with questions like:

* What did you have to do in order to play this game? (Listen, hear each answer, think, imagine, follow a line of reasoning, eliminate possibilities, etc.)

* Ask the person who finally solved the riddle, "Joanne, did you have help from others in finding the answer?" It nearly always comes out that the person relied on previous questions and answers. Use this to point out the interdependence of players, and reduce competition within the group to be the "winner".

* When do you see yourself having to use the kind of thinking you use in this game?

Usually a group of youngsters will be eager to try a second game right away.

Some important points to remember:

1. Immediately following the telling of each story and before the questioning begins, ask if anyone in the group has heard it before and knows the answer. Tell these people to observe and refrain from questioning.

2. Use the "does not compute" response whenever a single word or phrase in a question makes it impossible to answer with a "yes" or "no" answer. Examples from the story above:

- "Why does he live on the twentieth floor?" "Why" questions, as well as "where, who, when or which", cannot be answered "yes" or "no".

- "Does the elevator operator make him get off at the fifteenth floor?" No mention was made of an operator.

3. If a game goes past 10 or 12 minutes and some people begin to lose interest close the game for the present. There is absolutely nothing harmful in leaving the puzzle unsolved. The group can return to it another time, when interest and energy are high. Some students may protest, but do not give the answer. The experience of non-closure provides some valuable learning in itself; but more importantly, once a group has expended considerable energy on the game, the victory should be an earned one. Although there may be some unusual circumstances under which you would give the group the answer, I have found it best not to do so (even if some are begging). The point here is not to "take the answer away by giving it." You can always return to it later. What is important is that the students earn the feeling of "we-did-it!"

4. Share the computer (leader) role. Once kids have learned how the game works, have a volunteer lead the game. He or she must choose from the stories he

or she already knows. As soon as you are convinced the student is familiar with the story, the answer, and the process (which you should previously have modeled) have the leader read the story to the class, and begin taking questions. Most important here is what you model. A child-led computer game is an excellent small-group activity to have going on while you are occupied elsewhere in the classroom.

5. You may periodically want to encourage categorical thinking. When a player asks a question beginning, "Would it help us to know…" or "Does it have anything to do with…" pause in the game and show how the type of question is uniquely helpful in narrowing down the range of questions, distilling and focusing the group's attention, or cutting away large slices of the topic that are irrelevant. Thus, the question "Is David's occupation important?" tends to be more useful than "Is he a plumber? A teacher?", etc.

6. Be sure that a question is exactly true, or exactly false, before responding. One word can make the difference.

1. The Powerful Meal

A wife gave her husband a single item of food. He died* as a result of eating it, and even though thousands of people heard of it, the wife was never brought to trial.

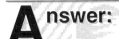

Answer:

The wife was Eve; the husband, Adam.

*The frequency of death and dying in these stories is perhaps attributable to the probable origin of the genre in crime novels. The game fun tends to focus more on the process (such as listening, thinking, asking, combining and eliminating elements, etc.) rather than content. I have never flinched at sharing the stories with children. The teacher will make choices to use the stories as is, or modify them, according to his or her own comfort level.

2. The Masked Man

The man was afraid to go home, because the man with the mask was there.

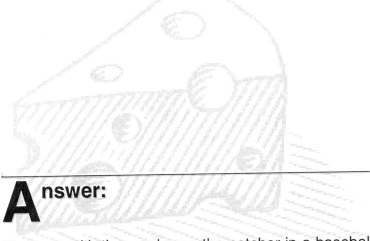

Answer:

The man with the mask was the catcher in a baseball game; the other man was a base-runner.

3. The Skiing Accident

Mr. Allen was reading a newspaper, and came across an article about the death of a woman in the Swiss Alps. Reading that a Dr. Jones' wife had accidentally fallen to her death while skiing, Mr. Allen went to the police and told them, "Jones murdered his wife." After questioning, Dr. Jones confessed to the crime. How did Mr. Allen know?

Answer:

Mr. Allen was a travel agent. He remembered selling Jones one round-trip ticket and one one-way ticket to Switzerland.

4. John and Mary

John and Mary are on the floor. There are pieces of broken glass and a puddle of liquid on the floor also. Mary is dead.

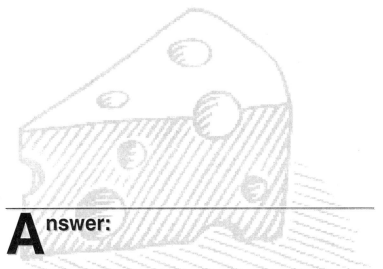

Answer:

John, a cat, knocked over the fishbowl of Mary, a fish.

4

5. The Armed Proprietor

A young woman walked into a café and asked for a drink of water. The man behind the counter suddenly pulled out a gun and pointed it at her. A few seconds elapsed, and then the woman smiled, thanked the man, and left.

Answer:

She had the hiccups, and was frightened out of them.

6. The Sawdust Mystery

If the man had seen the sawdust, he wouldn't have died.

Answer:

The man who was blind made his living in the circus as a midget clown. Termites had been eating the end of his cane, causing the sawdust. Because he could not see that the cane had become shorter, when he had to reach down farther than usual to touch the ground with it, he thought he was growing. Thinking this would result in his losing his job, he became despondent, and shot himself.

Note: This solution must be reached in parts, rather than all at once.

6

7. The Mysterious Suicide

A man's dead body hangs from a rope tied to the center of a ceiling beam in a large, empty room. His feet are ten feet from the floor. No other items are in the room. The man killed himself by hanging.

Answer:

He climbed a stack of dry ice, attached the rope, and then waited for the ice to evaporate.

8. The Car Trunk Mystery

A gang of thieves robs a warehouse one night. They capture two night watchmen and place them, unharmed and unbound, in the trunk of a car parked nearby. The next morning, when employees hear sounds coming from the trunk, they open it. One man steps out, alive and well. The other is dead.

Answer:

The survivor breathed the air from the spare tire.

9. 53 Bicycles

A man lies dead in a room with 53 bicycles also in the room.

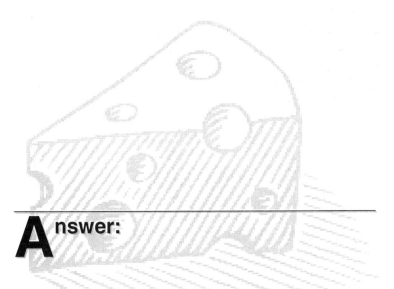

Answer:

The man had been playing cards for money. He had cheated by pulling an extra ace from his sleeve. His opponent had shot him and fled. The "bicycles" are bicycle cards.

10. Cause of Death Known

A forensic policeman was called to examine the body of a man lying by the roadside, dead. The dead man was wearing a knapsack. There were no marks on the body or blood anywhere. The policeman could immediately determine the cause of death.

Answer:

The "knapsack" was an unopened parachute.

10

11. Crazy Aunt Mabel

George lived with his Aunt Mabel, whose sanity he sometimes doubted. One day, Aunt Mabel was bragging about what an expert she had been in her former line of work. "I'll just go and get my clippings and show you," she said. When she returned, George took one look, called the authorities, and had her committed.

Answer:

Mabel had been a barber. She had saved actual hair clippings all these years.

12. Doctor's Dilemma

A doctor was driving his son to school one day when their car was rammed by a truck. The doctor was killed and the son was seriously injured in the accident. The son was rushed to a nearby hospital and prepared for surgery. However, when they wheeled him into surgery, the surgeon announced, "I can't operate! This is my own son!"

Answer:

The surgeon was the boy's mother.

13. Identical Drinks

Don and Dan enter a tavern and are served identical drinks. Don drinks his quickly, and feels fine. Dan drinks his very slowly and dies.

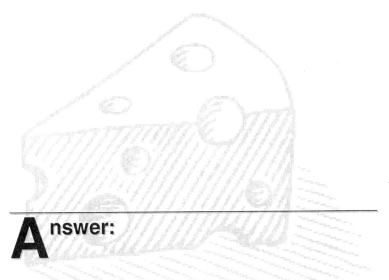

Answer:

There was poison in the ice.

14. Important Phone Call

"Oh, what have I done!" yelled the woman, as the phone rang.

Answer:

The woman, lonely and despondent, had sat by her phone for months, hoping for a friendly call but never receiving even one. Finally, out of despair she jumped out of her 20th story apartment window—just as the phone rang.

14

15. Murder in Public

A murder was committed before thousands of people, but all of them thought it was an accident.

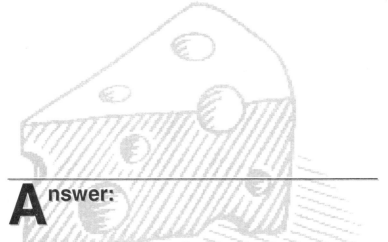

Answer:

A trapeze artist who took his cues from the organist for when to start, reach, and land, fell to his death. The organist had purposely changed the tempo in mid-act to throw him off.

16. No Bullet Holes

A man has been murdered while sitting in the driver's seat of a car. Although there are numerous bullet wounds in the body, and all the doors and windows of the car are tightly closed and locked, there are no bullet-holes anywhere in the car.

Answer:

The car is a convertible and the top is down.

17. Albatross Soup

Horton walked into a restaurant and read on the menu: Albatross Soup. "My favorite!" he cried, and ordered a double-portion. The waiter brought the soup, and when Horton tasted it, he screamed and fainted.

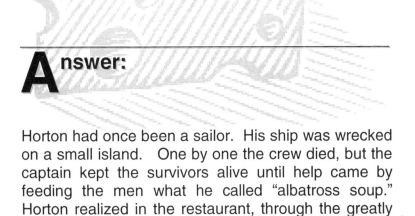

Answer:

Horton had once been a sailor. His ship was wrecked on a small island. One by one the crew died, but the captain kept the survivors alive until help came by feeding the men what he called "albatross soup." Horton realized in the restaurant, through the greatly different taste of the real albatross soup, that he had once eaten human flesh!

18. Amazon Amazement

One hundred people were traveling down the Amazon on a flatboat when the boat, in calm water, capsized and all were drowned.

Answer:

A huge snake was spotted, hanging over the river from a free branch. The passengers panicked and all of them ran to one side to get away, capsizing the boat.

19. A Disastrous Party

A famous scientist was awarded a government prize for his invention of a new weapon. He decided to invite a number of his friends to a party in his laboratory. For entertainment he provided a juggler, an opera soprano, and a ballet dancer. At the height of the evening, all present were suddenly and mysteriously killed.

Answer:

The soprano sang a high note, exploding a glass beaker of lethal gas—the new weapon.

20. Another Disastrous Party

Sylvester had just received a promotion in his company. To celebrate, Sylvester and his wife invited his boss, his boss's wife and a party of seventy for dinner. A fire broke out during the party and no one escaped from the room. In the morning, firemen found the bodies of only five people in the ruins.

Answer:

There were never more than five people there: the man, his wife, his boss, his boss's wife, and the "party of 70" –an elderly relative.

ABOUT THE AUTHOR

Nathan Levy

Nathan Levy is the author of more than 40 books which have sold almost 250,000 copies to teachers and parents in the US, Europe, Asia, South America, Australia and Africa. His unique <u>Stories with Holes</u> series continues to be proclaimed the most popular activity used in gifted, special education and regular classrooms by hundreds of educators. An extremely popular, dynamic speaker on thinking, writing and differentiation, Nathan is in high demand as a workshop leader in school and business settings. As a former school principal, company president, parent of four daughters and management trainer, Nathan's ability to transfer knowledge and strategies to audiences through humorous, thought provoking stories assures that participants leave with a plethora of new ways to approach their future endeavors.

NL Associates is pleased to be the publisher of this book. Teachers, students and other readers are invited to contribute their own "Stories with Holes" for possible inclusion in future volumes. Suggested stories will not be returned to you and will be acknowledged only if selected. Please send your suggestions to:

NL Associates Inc
PO Box 1199
Hightstown NJ 08520-0399
www.storieswithholes.com

21

Dynamic Speakers
Creative Workshops
Relevant Topics

Nathan Levy, author of the <u>Stories with Holes</u> series and <u>There Are Those</u>, and other nationally known authors and speakers, can help your school or organization achieve positive results with children. We can work with you to provide a complete in-service package or have one of our presenters lead one of several informative and entertaining workshops.

Workshop Topics Include:

- Practical Activities for Teaching Gifted Children
- Differentiating in the Regular Classroom
- How to Help Children Read, Write and Think Better
- Using <u>Stories with Holes</u> and Other Thinking Activities
- Powerful Strategies to Enhance Learning
- Communicating Better in the Workplace
- Communicating Better at Home
- Communicating Better at School
- The Principal as an Educational Leader
                and many more…